IMAM HASAN (A)

4

HEAVENLY CHILDREN
The Intelligent Boy

D1712769

Kisa Kids Publications

Dedication

This book is dedicated to the beloved Imām of our time (AJ). May Allāh (swt) hasten his reappearance and help to become his true companions.

Acknowledgements

Prophet Muḥammad (s): The pen of a writer is mightier than the blood of a martyr.

True reward lies with Allāh, but we would like to sincerely thank the efforts of Shaykh Salim Yusufali, Brother Aliakb Shaheidari, Sisters Sabika Mithani, Fatemah Mithani, Amna Hussain, Asieh Zarghami, Zahra Sabur, Sajeda Mercha Kisae Nazar, Sarah Assaf, Nadia Dossani, Fathema Abidi, Fatemeh Eslami, Fatima Hussain, Fatemah Megh Sukaena Kalyan, and Zehra Abbas. We would especially like to thank Nainava Publications for their contribution May Allāh bless them in this world and the next.

Preface

Prophet Muḥammad (s): Nurture and raise your children in the best way. Raise them with the love of the Prophe and the Ahlul Bayt (a).

Literature is an influential form of media that often shapes the thoughts and views of an entire generation. Therefo in order to establish an Islāmic foundation for the future generations, there is a dire need for compelling Islam literature. Over the past several years, this need has become increasingly prevalent throughout Islāmic centers a schools everywhere. Due to the growing dissonance between parents, children, society, and the teachings of Islā and the Ahlul Bayt (a), this need has become even more pressing. Al-Kisa Foundation, along with its subsidiary, Ki Kids Publications, was conceived in an effort to help bridge this gap with the guidance of ʿulamah and the help educators. We would like to make this a communal effort and platform. Therefore, we sincerely welcome constructi feedback and help in any capacity.

The goal of the *Heavenly Children* series is to foster the love of Ahlul Bayt (a) in children and to help them establi the 14 Maʿṣūmīn as their role models. We hope that you and your children enjoy these books and use them as means to achieve this goal, inshāʾAllāh.

We pray to Allāh to give us the strength and *tawfīq* to perform our duties and responsibilities.

With Duʾās,
Nabi R. Mir (Abidi)

Disclaimer: Religious texts have *not* been translated verbatim so as to meet the developmental and comprehensi needs of children.

Kisa Kids Publications
4415 Fortran Court
San Jose, CA 95134
(260) KISA-KID [547-2543]

To prepare for their ziyarat trip, Ahmad, his Mama, and his Baba were remembering all of the fourteen Ma'soomeen. Mama had just finished telling Ahmad about Sayyidah Fatimah (a).

"So, Prophet Muhammad (s) and Sayyidah Fatimah (a) are in Medina… Is anyone else there for us to visit?" Ahmad asked his parents.

"Well," Mama said, "there is a special cemetery in Medina called Jannatul Baqi. Four of our Imams and many other great people are buried there. One of the Imams buried there is Imam Hasan (a), the eldest son of Imam Ali (a) and Sayyidah Fatimah (a)."

"Oh, I remember you told me about Imam Hasan (a)! Everyone was very happy when he was born!" Ahmad grinned.

Mama nodded. "Yes, that's right! And he was born on the 15th of Ramadhan. He was very special to his grandfather, Prophet Muhammad (s). The Prophet (s) used to carry him on his shoulders and tell everyone that Imam Hasan (a) and his brother, Imam Husain (a), are the leaders of the youth of paradise!"

"Even I love to ride on my grandfather's shoulders," Ahmad said laughing. "And his grandfather was the real Prophet Muhammad (s)! He must have been very special."

"Imam Hasan (a) was a very special person, indeed. He was the flagbearer of Imam Ali's (a) army in many big battles, like the Battles of Siffin, Jamal, and Nahrawan. This means that he would hold up the army's flag. In a battle, this is a very important job. He was also strong and brave, just like his father! After Imam Ali (a) was martyred, Imam Hasan (a) became the second Imam," Baba explained.

"Did Imam Hasan (a) become shaheed* in one of those battles?" asked Ahmad.

"No," said Mama, "Actually, he was poisoned by his wife, Ja'dah bint** Ash'ath. He was martyred on the 28th of Safar."

Ahmad was stunned! "That is very wrong," said Ahmad.

"Yes it is, but Imam Hasan (a) lived a very great life. Even as a child, he had great qualities and loved knowledge! Let me tell you a great story about his childhood!" Baba said.

*Shaheed: someone who dies in the path of Allah
**Daughter of

1

The bright sunshine poured into the Prophet's masjid, illuminating a hall packed with people lined in prayer. At the head of the congregation was the Noble Prophet of Allah (s). The Prophet (s) uttered the final salaam, raised his hands to his ears, and recited "Allahu Akbar" as he finished leading the prayer. Then, he slowly made his way towards the mimbar* to address the crowd. Everyone began settling down.

*Mimbar: a pulpit where the Imam sits to address a crowd

In a small corner near the back of the masjid, a five-year-old boy sat, intently waiting for the speech. Even at such a young age, the boy seemed ready to pay attention. This beautiful child was none other than the Prophet's grandson, Imam Hasan (a).

The Prophet (s) began his sermon. He spoke about the verses of the Quran that had just been revealed. His loyal followers beamed, humbled to receive this valuable knowledge. In fact, they were thrilled just to be sitting before the Prophet of Islam (s). It was such an honor. The Prophet's heavenly voice brought out the beauty of Allah's words even more.

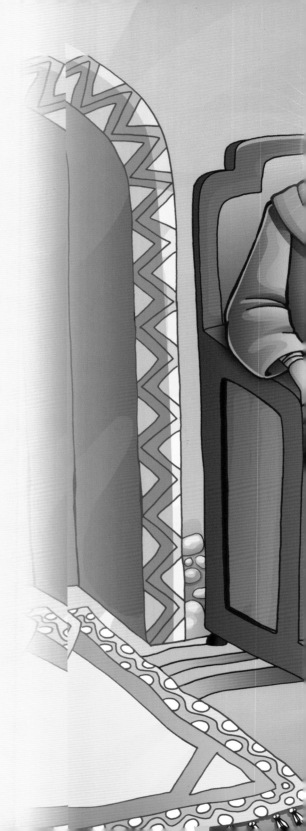

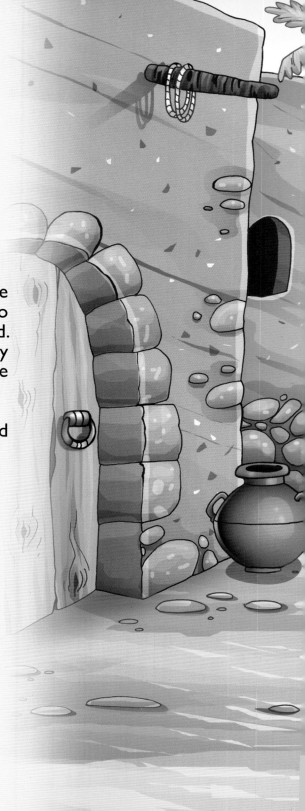

The Prophet's powerful speech echoed throughout the masjid. Everyone listened in awe. As his sermon came to an end, he recited a du'a, and the congregation dispersed. Some people began to leave the masjid. Others patiently stood in line, waiting to shake and kiss the hand of the Noble Prophet (s).

Little Imam Hasan (a) slipped through the crowd and excitedly ran home as soon as the sermon ended.

Imam Hasan (a) burst through the front door of his home. His mother, Sayyidah Fatimah (a), kneeled down and opened her arms as her son ran into them.

She looked at the young boy affectionately, waiting to hear what he had to say. Just as he always did, he began telling his mother about all the beautiful new verses he had learned from the Noble Prophet (s) that day. Sayyidah Fatimah (a) listened to him attentively and encouraged him to continue with each verse he recited. They sat together, talking about Allah.

A few hours later, Imam Ali (a) returned home. Sayyidah Fatimah Zahra (a) warmly greeted her husband, "Salaamun Alaikum." She handed him a glass of water.

Imam Ali (a) lovingly replied, "Wa Alaikum Salaam," and thanked Allah and her for the water.

As he rested, Sayyidah Fatimah (a) began to tell him about the new verses that the Prophet of Allah (s) had spoken about. Surprised, Imam Ali (a) asked, "How did you know about these verses?"

Sayyidah Fatimah (a) smiled widely and said, "Our son Hasan recited these beautiful verses for me!"

Imam Ali (a) smiled in admiration of Imam Hasan (a). He knew that Imam Hasan (a) was an intelligent child, but he wanted to hear him recite these verses with his own ears. He was amazed at how such a young child could memorize all those verses after hearing them at just one occasion!

Imam Ali (a) had an idea. If he came home early, he could hear Imam Hasan (a) tell his mother about the Prophet's sermon! It would amuse and amaze him so much to hear this beautiful conversation between Imam Hasan (a) and his mother.

The next day, after the Noble Prophet (s) finished leading the prayer, Imam Hasan (a) once again nestled in a small corner in the back. After the sermon was over, Imam Hasan (a) tried to leave the masjid quickly, but the back entrance was too crowded.

Just as he had planned, Imam Ali (a) was able to get home before him.

Imam Ali (a) reached the house and greeted Sayyidah Fatimah (a). He then searched for the perfect hiding spot, a place where he could hear his son enter but remain hidden. There was a doorway with a curtain. Imam Ali (a) quietly hid behind it.

Soon, Imam Hasan (a) entered the house, and as usual, ran to hug his dear mother.

Sayyidah Fatimah (a) gave him a kiss on the cheek. She asked, "My dear son, what did you learn from the Prophet of Allah (s) today?"

Imam Hasan (a) opened his mouth to speak, but something strange happened! No matter how hard he tried explaining the verses to his mother, he kept stammering over his words.

Again, he tried, but it was useless! He couldn't get his words straight. "What happened, my dear son?" his mother asked. "You come home everyday and recite the verses to me so beautifully. Is something wrong?"

Imam Hasan (a) smiled shyly. "Dear mother, I feel the presence of a great and honorable person in this room. Because of his greatness, I have become tongue-tied!" He looked around the house curiously. *Who could be home,* he wondered.

Imam Ali (a) peeked out from behind the curtain and looked at his son. When the young boy saw his father, he suddenly understood!

Imam Ali (a) laughed heartily. He came out from behind the curtain and lovingly hugged and kissed his son. Although he did not get to hear his son recount the verses to Sayyidah Fatimah (a), Imam Ali (a) was still pleased. He was proud that his son was so passionate to learn and spread the words of the Quran.

Ḥayāt al-Imām al-Ḥasan bin ʿAlī (A), P. 59